Contents

Grilled Picante BBQ Chicken

Makes 6 servings

Prep Time: 5 minutes   Cook Time: 15 minutes

- $^3/_4$ cup Pace® Picante Sauce
- $^1/_4$ cup barbecue sauce
- 6 skinless, boneless chicken breast halves

1. Stir the picante sauce and barbecue sauce in a small bowl. Reserve all but $^1/_2$ **cup** picante sauce mixture to serve with the chicken.

2. Lightly oil the grill rack and heat the grill to medium. Grill the chicken for 15 minutes or until it's cooked through, turning and brushing often with the remaining picante sauce mixture. Discard any remaining picante sauce mixture.

3. Serve the chicken with the reserved picante sauce mixture.

Kitchen Tip

This simple basting sauce also makes a zesty dipping sauce for chicken wings or nuggets.

Pasta Primavera

Makes 4 servings

Prep Time: 5 minutes   Cook Time: 25 minutes

---

3 cups *uncooked* corkscrew-shaped pasta (rotini)

1 bag (16 ounces) frozen vegetable combination (broccoli, cauliflower, carrots)

1 jar (1 pound 10 ounces) Prego® Traditional Italian Sauce

Grated Parmesan cheese

1. Prepare pasta according to package directions in a 4-quart saucepan. Add the vegetables during the last 5 minutes of the cooking time. Drain the pasta and vegetables in a colander and return them to the saucepan.

2. Stir the Italian sauce into the saucepan. Heat, stirring occasionally, until hot and bubbling. Top with the cheese.

Creamy Souper Rice

Makes 4 servings

Prep Time: 5 minutes   Cook Time: 10 minutes   Stand Time: 5 minutes

1 can (10³/₄ ounces) Campbell's® Condensed Cream of Mushroom Soup (Regular *or* 98% Fat Free)

1¹/₂ cups Swanson® Chicken Broth (Regular, Natural Goodness® *or* Certified Organic)

1¹/₂ cups *uncooked* instant white rice

1 tablespoon grated Parmesan cheese

Freshly ground black pepper

1. Heat the soup and broth in a 2-quart saucepan over medium heat to a boil.

2. Stir the rice and cheese in the saucepan. Cover the saucepan and remove from the heat. Let stand for 5 minutes. Fluff the rice with a fork. Serve with the black pepper and additional Parmesan cheese.

Kitchen Tip

Any of Campbell's® Condensed Cream Soups will work in this recipe: Cream of Chicken, Cream of Celery, even Cheddar Cheese.

French Onion Burgers

Makes 4 servings

Prep Time: 5 minutes   Cook Time: 20 minutes

---

   1   pound ground beef

   1   can (10½ ounces) Campbell's® Condensed French Onion Soup

   4   slices Swiss cheese

   4   round hard rolls, split

1. Shape the beef into **4** (½-inch-thick) burgers.

2. Heat a 10-inch skillet over medium-high heat. Add the burgers and cook until they're well browned on both sides. Remove the burgers from the skillet. Pour off any fat.

3. Stir the soup in the skillet and heat to a boil. Return the burgers to the skillet. Reduce the heat to low. Cover and cook for 5 minutes or until the burgers are cooked through. Top the burgers with the cheese and cook until the cheese is melted. Serve the burgers in the rolls with the soup mixture.

Kitchen Tip

You can also serve these burgers in a bowl atop a mound of hot mashed potatoes, with some of the onion gravy poured over.

Sicilian-Style Pizza

Makes 8 servings

Thaw Time: 3 hours   Prep Time: 10 minutes   Bake Time: 25 minutes

2   loaves (1 pound *each*) frozen white bread dough

Vegetable cooking spray

1³/₄ cups Prego® Traditional Italian Sauce

2   cups shredded mozzarella cheese (about 8 ounces)

1. Thaw the bread dough according to the package directions. Heat the oven to 375°F. Spray a 15×10-inch jellyroll pan with cooking spray. Place the dough loaves into the pan. Press the dough from the center out until it covers the bottom of the pan. Pinch the edges of the dough to form a rim.

2. Spread the sauce over the crust. Top with the cheese.

3. Bake for 25 minutes or until the cheese is melted and the crust is golden.

Kitchen Tip

To thaw the dough more quickly, place the dough into a microwavable dish. Brush with melted butter or spray with vegetable cooking spray. Microwave on LOW for 1 to 2 minutes.

Chocolate Goldfish® Pretzel Clusters

Makes 1 pound

Prep Time: 5 minutes   *Cook Time: 1 minute*   *Chill Time: 30 minutes*

 1 package (12 ounces) semi-sweet chocolate pieces (about 2 cups)

2½ cups Pepperidge Farm® Pretzel Goldfish®

 1 container (4 ounces) multi-colored nonpareils

1. Line a baking sheet with waxed paper. Place the chocolate into a microwavable bowl. Microwave on HIGH for 1 minute. Stir. Microwave at 15-second intervals, stirring after each, until the chocolate is melted and smooth. Add the Goldfish® and stir to coat.

2. Drop the chocolate mixture by tablespoonfuls onto the baking sheet. Sprinkle the clusters with the nonpareils.

3. Refrigerate for 30 minutes or until the clusters are firm. Store in the refrigerator.

Kitchen Tip

To wrap for gift-giving, arrange the clusters in small candy box lined with colored plastic wrap.

Beef Steak with Sautéed Onions

Makes 8 servings

Prep Time: 5 minutes   *Cook Time: 25 minutes*

2 tablespoons olive oil

2 large onions, thinly sliced (about 2 cups)

2 pounds boneless beef sirloin steak, strip *or* rib steaks, cut into 8 pieces

1 jar (16 ounces) Pace® Picante Sauce

1. Heat *1 tablespoon* of the oil in a 12-inch skillet over medium heat. Add the onions and cook until they're tender. Remove the onions from the skillet and keep warm.

2. Heat the remaining oil in the skillet. Add the steak pieces and cook until they're well browned on both sides.

3. Add the picante sauce and return the onions to the skillet. Cook for 3 minutes for medium-rare or until desired doneness.

Italian Cheeseburger Pasta

Makes 4 servings

Prep Time: 5 minutes   Cook Time: 35 minutes

1 pound ground beef

1 jar (1 pound 10 ounces) Prego® Traditional Italian Sauce

2 cups water

2 cups *uncooked* corkscrew-shaped pasta (rotini)

½ cup shredded mozzarella cheese

1. Cook the beef in a 10-inch skillet over medium-high heat until well browned, stirring frequently to separate meat. Pour off any fat.

2. Stir the Italian sauce, water and pasta into the skillet. Heat to a boil. Reduce the heat to medium. Cook and stir for 25 minutes or until the pasta is tender but still firm. Sprinkle with the cheese.

Polenta au Gratin

Makes 6 servings

Prep Time: 10 minutes   Bake Time: 25 minutes   Stand Time: 5 minutes

- 1 cup Pace® Picante Sauce
- 1 package (18 ounces) prepared polenta, cut into $\frac{1}{2}$-inch slices
- 4 green onions, minced (about $\frac{1}{2}$ cup)
- 1$\frac{1}{2}$ cups shredded Mexican cheese blend (about 6 ounces)

1. Heat the oven to 350°F. Spread *$\frac{1}{2}$ cup* picante sauce on the bottom of a 2-quart shallow baking dish. Layer the polenta slices, overlapping slightly, in the baking dish. Top with the green onions, remaining picante sauce and cheese.

2. Bake for 25 minutes or until the polenta is golden brown and the cheese is melted. Let stand for 5 minutes.

Sirloin Steak Olé

Makes 6 servings

Prep Time: 5 minutes   Grill Time: 20 minutes   Stand Time: 10 minutes

1 boneless beef sirloin steak *or* top round steak, 1$\frac{1}{2}$-inches thick (about 1$\frac{1}{2}$ pounds)

1 jar (16 ounces) Pace® Picante Sauce

1. Lightly oil the grill rack and heat the grill to medium. Grill the steak for 20 minutes for medium-rare or to desired doneness, turning the steak over halfway through grilling and brushing often with *1 cup* picante sauce.

2. Let stand for 10 minutes before slicing. Serve with additional picante sauce.

2-Step Nacho Pasta

Makes 4 servings

Prep Time: 5 minutes   Cook Time: 15 minutes

1 can (11 ounces) Campbell's® Condensed Fiesta Nacho Cheese Soup

½ cup milk

4 cups corkscrew-shaped pasta (rotini), cooked and drained

1. Heat the soup and milk in a 2-quart saucepan over medium heat. Cook until hot and bubbling.

2. Stir in the pasta. Cook and stir until hot.

Power Breakfast Sandwiches

Makes 2 sandwiches

Prep Time: 5 minutes

- ¼ cup peanut butter
- 4 slices Pepperidge Farm® Stone Ground 100% Whole Wheat
- ¼ cup raisins
- 1 medium banana, sliced

Spread the peanut butter on **4** bread slices. Divide the raisins and banana between **2** bread slices. Top with the remaining bread slices, peanut butter-side down. Cut the sandwiches in half.

Kitchen Tip

*Substitute **1** large apple, cored and sliced, for the raisins and banana.*

Pizza Fries

Makes 8 servings

Prep Time: 20 minutes   Bake Time: 5 minutes

1 bag (2 pounds) frozen French fries

1 cup Prego® Traditional Italian Sauce, any variety

1½ cups shredded mozzarella cheese (about 6 ounces)

   Diced pepperoni (optional)

1. Prepare the fries according to the package directions. Remove from the oven. Pour the sauce over the fries.

2. Top with the cheese and pepperoni, if desired.

3. Bake for 5 minutes or until the cheese is melted.

Cheeseburger Pasta

Makes 5 servings

Prep Time: 5 minutes   Cook Time: 20 minutes

1 pound ground beef

1 can (10³/₄ ounces) Campbell's® Condensed Cheddar Cheese Soup

1 can (10³/₄ ounces) Campbell's® Condensed Tomato Soup (Regular *or* Healthy Request®)

1¹/₂ cups water

2 cups *uncooked* medium shell-shaped pasta

1. Cook the beef in a 10-inch skillet over medium-high heat until it's well browned, stirring often to separate meat. Pour off any fat.

2. Stir the soups, water and pasta in the skillet and heat to a boil. Reduce the heat to medium. Cook for 10 minutes or until the pasta is tender, stirring often.

Easy Beef & Pasta

Makes 4 servings

Prep Time: 5 minutes   Cook Time: 20 minutes

1   tablespoon vegetable oil

1   pound boneless beef sirloin steak, $^3/_4$-inch thick, cut into very thin
     strips

1   can (10$^3/_4$ ounces) Campbell's® Condensed Tomato Soup (Regular *or*
     Healthy Request®)

$^1/_2$ cup water

1   bag (about 16 ounces) frozen vegetable pasta blend

1. Heat the oil in a 10-inch skillet over medium-high heat. Add the beef and cook until it's well browned, stirring often. Pour off any fat.

2. Stir the soup, water and vegetable pasta blend in the skillet and heat to a boil. Reduce the heat to low. Cover and cook for 5 minutes or until the beef is cooked through.